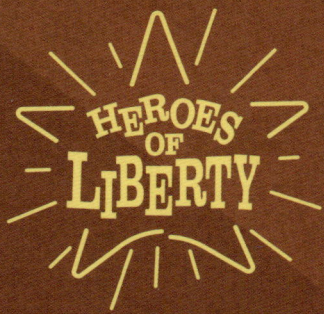

American values, one story at a time.

Joyce Claiborne-West

Mark Twain – Writing the American Story

Illustrations by Carl Pearce

Text copyright © Heroes of Liberty Inc., 2022

Illustrations copyright Heroes of Liberty Inc., 2022

1216 Broadway, New York, NY 10001

All rights reserved. No part of this book may be reproduced or transmitted in any form or by any means, electronic or mechanical, including photocopying, recording, or by any information storage and retrieval system without written permission from the publisher.

Heroes of Liberty Inc.
1216 Broadway, New York, NY 10001

Find more heroes to read about on:
WWW.HEROESOFLIBERTY.COM

Mark Twain

WRITING THE AMERICAN STORY

Mark Twain

has been called the father of American literature. This is because his books capture deep things about the American soul: the soul of a people who dared to venture into the unknown, and to imagine and build a new nation out in the wilderness.

Mark Twain understood America's hopes and joys—and its fears too. His words made it all come alive: the big cities and the towns of the Wild West, the Rocky Mountains and Nevada deserts, the big lakes and the majestic forests. But above all, he loved the Mississippi River. He spent years on the Mississippi as the pilot of steam-powered riverboats.

For Mark Twain, life in America is always a great big adventure. This is why Americans of all ages love to read him to this day. Many see living in the country they love as a great adventure too.

Besides, he had a great sense of humor, and everyone likes a good laugh.

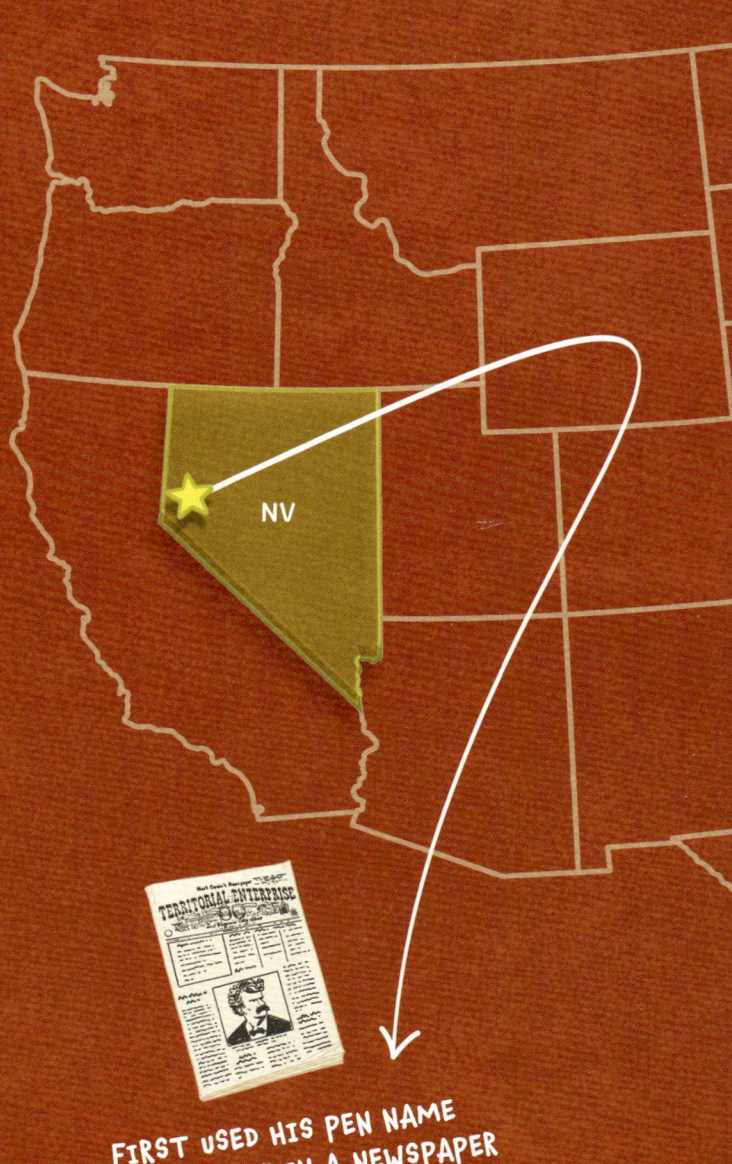

FIRST USED HIS PEN NAME "MARK TWAIN" IN A NEWSPAPER FEBRUARY 3, 1863
VIRGINIA CITY, NEVADA

Mark Twain wasn't born as Mark Twain. He was born as Samuel Langhorne Clemens. He was born two months prematurely, on November 30, 1835. He was so small that his parents didn't think he'd survive; this was before hospitals had today's means to save babies born that early.

The Clemenses lived in a small Missouri village called Florida out in the wilderness. There were only a few dozen families in Florida back then. Now there are none. The place has since been deserted.

From early on, Sammy—as he was called when he was little—would listen to the sounds of the night. They seemed to promise adventure and danger.

Frogs croaking, crickets chirping, winds whistling, and dogs howling—all of these would sometimes sound as close as if they were just outside his window, and sometimes small and distant in the deep, great big silence of the night.

Even as a toddler, little Sammy had his own funny way of looking at things. "The dog has a tail bebind," he once informed his family. He had meant to say, "behind." "The cat also has a tail bebind," he said. "And I haven't any tail bebind at all!"

His uncle, John, decided to fix this and pinned a paper tail to the back of Sammy's pants.

There was one plantation in Florida, Missouri back then, and its owner had slaves. One of these slaves was an old woman whom the children called "Aunt Hannah." The children believed she was a thousand years old. She had even known Moses, they said, and had seen the greatest, most evil slaveholder of all: the wicked Pharaoh, King of Egypt. Some even said she had seen the Egyptian army washed over by the sea when they had tried to chase Moses and the people of Israel. He never caught them, and they had escaped to freedom.

Aunt Hannah wasn't really a thousand years old. But she knew how to tell children spooky stories about witches and elves, about magic and wonder. And though he didn't know it yet, little Sammy first learned from Aunt Hannah the art that would make him famous one day: storytelling.

When Sammy was four years old, the family moved to the town of Hannibal, Missouri, on the banks of the Mississippi River. Hannibal would become the model for the imaginary town in which Mark Twain's two most famous novels would be set: *The Adventures of Tom Sawyer* and *The Adventures of Huckleberry Finn*. When he imagined Tom and Huck doing their mischief, playing in the woods, sneaking to the graveyard in the dead of night, or swimming in the Mississippi, this was where he imagined them.

When Sammy grew a little older, he began to explore his surroundings by day and by night. It was sometimes scary, but the possibility of adventure always beckoned.

Sammy shared a bedroom with his brother, Henry, on the second floor of the family home. Sometimes, in the dead of night, his friends would whistle to him from outside, imitating bird calls so that the adults wouldn't notice them. Sammy would get dressed in the dark, careful not to wake Henry up. He would crawl out of the window, then walk along a small ledge, jump onto the roof of a shed, and slide down from there onto the ground. He and his friends would then have their own secret nightly adventures. Sammy was very much like his Tom Sawyer. And like him, he often got into trouble.

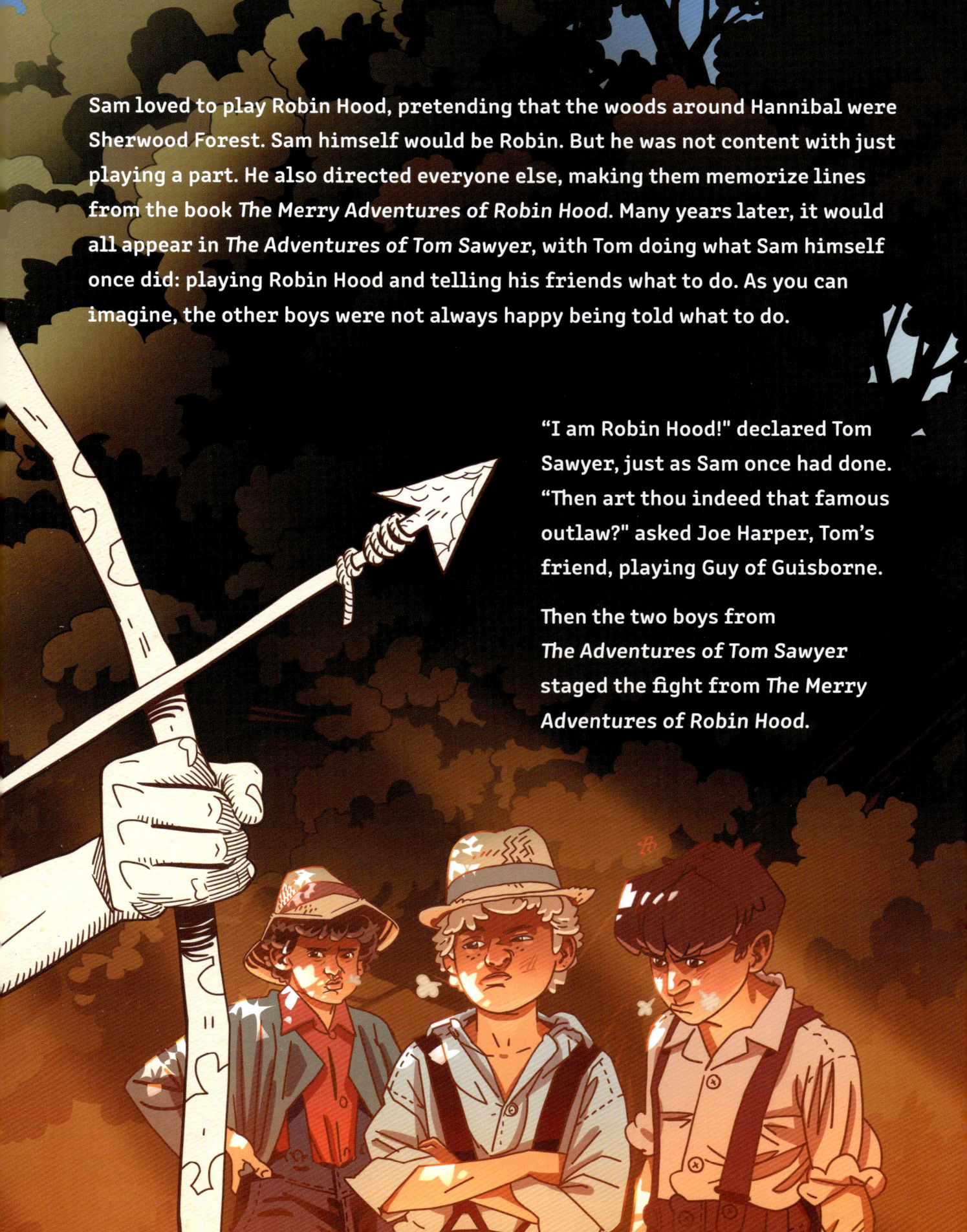

Sam loved to play Robin Hood, pretending that the woods around Hannibal were Sherwood Forest. Sam himself would be Robin. But he was not content with just playing a part. He also directed everyone else, making them memorize lines from the book *The Merry Adventures of Robin Hood*. Many years later, it would all appear in *The Adventures of Tom Sawyer*, with Tom doing what Sam himself once did: playing Robin Hood and telling his friends what to do. As you can imagine, the other boys were not always happy being told what to do.

"I am Robin Hood!" declared Tom Sawyer, just as Sam once had done. "Then art thou indeed that famous outlaw?" asked Joe Harper, Tom's friend, playing Guy of Guisborne.

Then the two boys from *The Adventures of Tom Sawyer* staged the fight from *The Merry Adventures of Robin Hood*.

But Tom's friend Joe refused to yield.
So Tom got angry and said, "Fall! Fall! Why don't you fall?"

"I shan't!" said Joe. "Why don't you fall yourself? You're getting the worst of it."
"Why, that ain't anything. I can't fall; that ain't the way it is in the book. The book says, 'Then with one back-handed stroke he slew poor Guy of Guisborne.' You're to turn around and let me hit you in the back."
There was no getting around the authorities, so Joe turned, received the whack, and fell. "Now," said Joe, getting up, "you got to let me kill you. That's fair."
"Why, I can't do that, it ain't in the book," said Tom.

All of this is in the book *The Adventures of Tom Sawyer*. When you read it one day, Tom Sawyer, Becky Thatcher, Aunt Polly, Huck Finn, and the rest of the gang will come alive for you too, like they have for so many children before you.

It was this book, along with *The Adventures of Huckleberry Finn*, that would make Sam—Mark Twain—a very famous writer—and not just in America, but all around the world.

Is Tom really just Sam when he was young? Did what's in the book really happen? Well, not exactly. Here's what Sam—Mark Twain—writes in the preface to the book:

"Most of the adventures recorded in this book really occurred; one or two were experiences of my own, the rest those of boys who were schoolmates of mine. Huck Finn is drawn from life; Tom Sawyer also, but not from an individual—he is a combination of the characteristics of three boys whom I knew."

But in one sense, it was very real. The purpose of the book, Mark Twain explained, is not just to entertain boys and girls. He hoped, he said, that adults would read it too. "Part of my plan," he wrote, "has been to try to pleasantly remind adults of what they once were themselves, and of how they felt and thought and talked, and what queer enterprises they sometimes engaged in."

Wouldn't it be nice if adults sometimes remembered how they felt when they were small, and understood better what their children feel and think? It would probably save everybody a whole lot of trouble!

HANNIBAL

TERMS:---One Dollar, if paid In Advance: If not
PUBLISHED BY O. CLEMENS, ON HILL ST, NEAR

NEW SERIES.---VOL. IV.. HANNI

DISASTER STRIKES

When Sam was just eleven years old, disaster struck. His father died of pneumonia, which was often deadly back then, before we had good hospitals and modern medicine. Sam eventually had to leave school and go to work to help the family get by. He became an apprentice in a print shop.

When his older brother, Orion, bought a small local newspaper, Sam helped him with the printing and also wrote some funny news stories to beef up the paper. Sam would eventually write for many newspapers later in life.

But for now, like most boys his age who grew up near the great Mississippi River, he wanted to be a riverboat pilot.

Young Samuel L. Cleme hard at work at the Jou

JOURNAL.

within Six Months, One Dollar and Fifty Cents

A FEW DOORS WEST OF SELMER BUILDING

, MO., FRIDAY, : : : : JUNE 1st, 1849.

The pilot of a riverboat was even more important than the boat's captain. He was a navigator who helped the captain steer the boat away from trouble. Mississippi riverboats could be huge and very hard to maneuver. They could be the length of a football field, and sometimes even more! The long river, with all its bends and islands, contained many hazards to the big, flat-bottomed boats: underwater rocks, shallow waters, sharp turns, and jagged banks. It was the pilot's job to learn all these obstacles, in the light of day and in the dark of night. It was up to him to make sure the captain knew to avoid them.

It took Sam two years to master the river. And the tuition he had to pay was so high that he had to take out a loan. He sailed up and down the mighty 1,200-mile river until he memorized every nook and cranny. Only then did he become a real professional pilot.

Being a river pilot, he would say, was as free as a person could ever hope to be: sailing aboard different boats, respected by all, and getting paid a handsome salary too. It was a dream come true!

The many hours he stood at the bridge of those big boats, breathing in the early morning air, or feeling the chill of the breeze at night, hearing the clacking of steam engines, or the crashing water at the ship's huge paddle wheel—these were among the happiest times Sam ever knew. The river that he loved would come to life in his books.

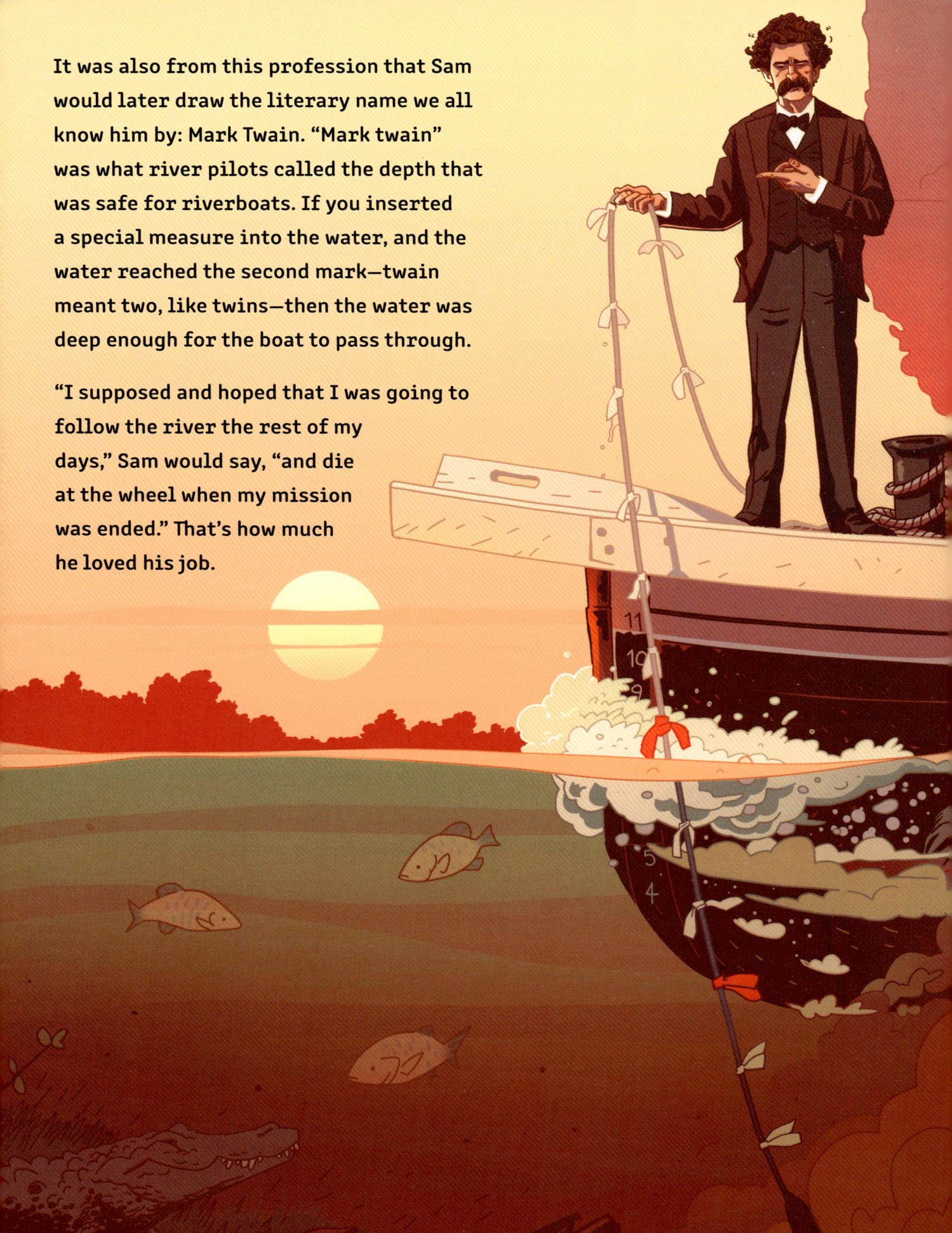

It was also from this profession that Sam would later draw the literary name we all know him by: Mark Twain. "Mark twain" was what river pilots called the depth that was safe for riverboats. If you inserted a special measure into the water, and the water reached the second mark—twain meant two, like twins—then the water was deep enough for the boat to pass through.

"I supposed and hoped that I was going to follow the river the rest of my days," Sam would say, "and die at the wheel when my mission was ended." That's how much he loved his job.

But it was not to be. In November 1860, Abraham Lincoln was elected president, and soon the South seceded from the Union. On April 12, 1861, the first shots were fired at Fort Sumter, and the Civil War began.

Travel on the Mississippi was blocked by the Union at the border that separated North from South. Sam's career as a river pilot was over.

It would take a while to see this as a blessing in disguise. If Sam had stayed a riverboat pilot, some of the greatest American literary treasures would probably never have been written.

When Sam's brother Orion was appointed secretary of the Nevada Territory, before Nevada became a state, Sam decided to join him and try his luck out in the Wild West.

For three weeks they traveled by stagecoach, bumping along the roads and sleeping on sacks of mail that the stagecoach carried out west. Sam would capture the experience in a book called *Roughing It*.

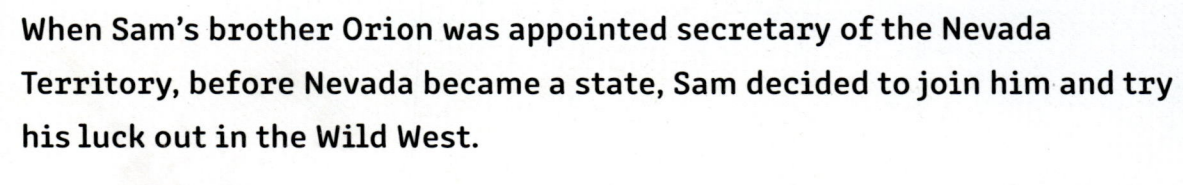

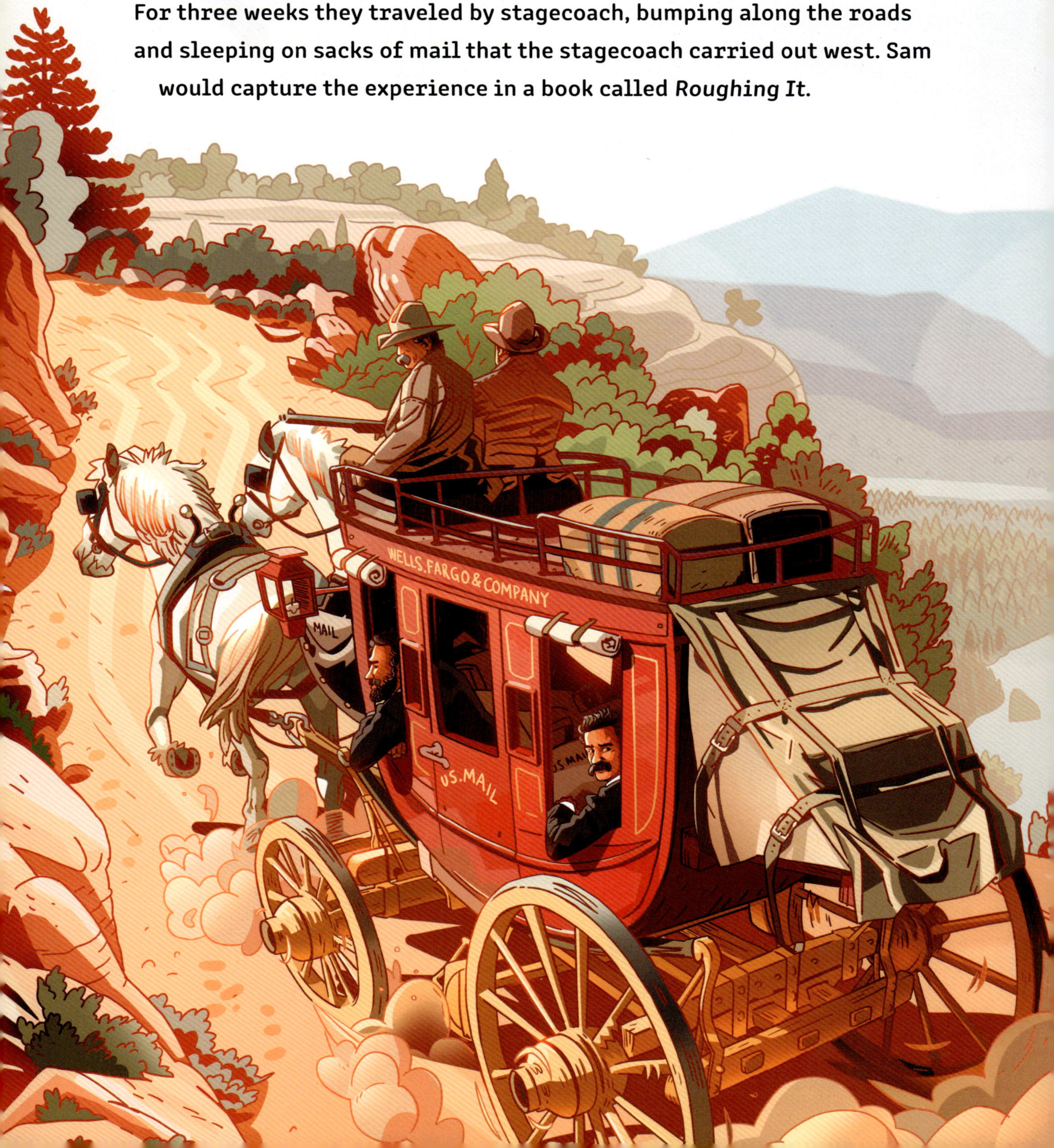

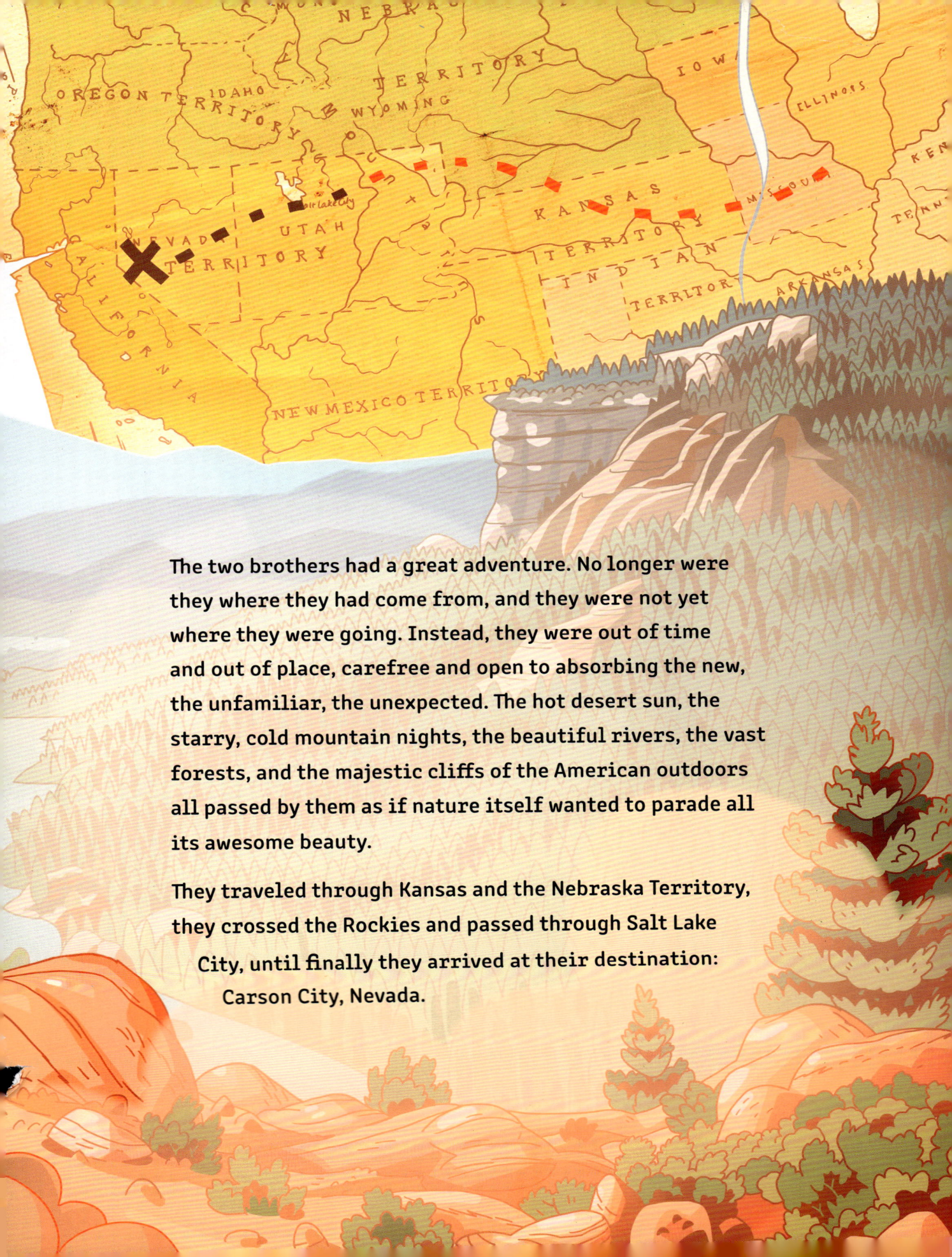

The two brothers had a great adventure. No longer were they where they had come from, and they were not yet where they were going. Instead, they were out of time and out of place, carefree and open to absorbing the new, the unfamiliar, the unexpected. The hot desert sun, the starry, cold mountain nights, the beautiful rivers, the vast forests, and the majestic cliffs of the American outdoors all passed by them as if nature itself wanted to parade all its awesome beauty.

They traveled through Kansas and the Nebraska Territory, they crossed the Rockies and passed through Salt Lake City, until finally they arrived at their destination: Carson City, Nevada.

There, Sam tried his hand at mining. The discovery of a huge silver deposit underground had inspired a gold rush to the area. Many hoped to get rich overnight if they found gold or silver in the earth. Few did, though. And Sam was not among the lucky, so he returned to the newspaper business. He settled in a miner's town called Virginia City, Nevada, where he took a full-time job as a writer for a local paper named the *Territorial Enterprise*.

Long before there were movies about the Wild West, Sam's writing captured its spirit and its sense of open opportunities, wild hopes, lawlessness, and often danger, too. He wrote about anything and everything: business, entertainment, crime, politics, gossip. As if writing with a permanent mischievous smile, he knew how to make his readers laugh, even as he also made them think. But what made Mark Twain famous throughout the United States was, believe it or not, a funny little story about a frog. Yes, a frog! And you can tell it is going to be funny by its name: *The Celebrated Jumping Frog of Calaveras County*

The story is about a man named Smiley, who loved to bet. He would bet on horse races and dog races, and he would have bet on cat races if there had been any to be found. If two birds were sitting on a fence, he would bet you which would fly first, and if he found a bug, he would bet you where it was going and how long it would take it to get there.

He would bet you on anything, and if he couldn't get you to bet against him, he would offer to switch and take your side of the bet.

And then one day, Smiley caught a frog and decided to teach it to jump. He had it practice day after day, until the frog could somersault and catch flies in the air. He called the frog Daniel Webster. And when he said, "Daniel, fly!" the frog would jump and catch a fly.

As you may have already guessed, Smiley had a plan. He would bet that his frog could jump higher than anyone else's frog.

The problem, of course, was that not many other people had frogs as pets. Do you know anyone who does?

One day, a stranger came to town. He ran into Smiley, who was carrying a box, and he asked him what was in it. Smiley told him it was a frog. And not just any frog. It was a jumping champion frog. He offered the stranger $40 in a bet that his frog could outjump the stranger's frog.

But of course, the stranger had no frog.

"That's alright," Smiley said, "if you'll hold my box a minute, I'll go and get you a frog." And off he went to find one.

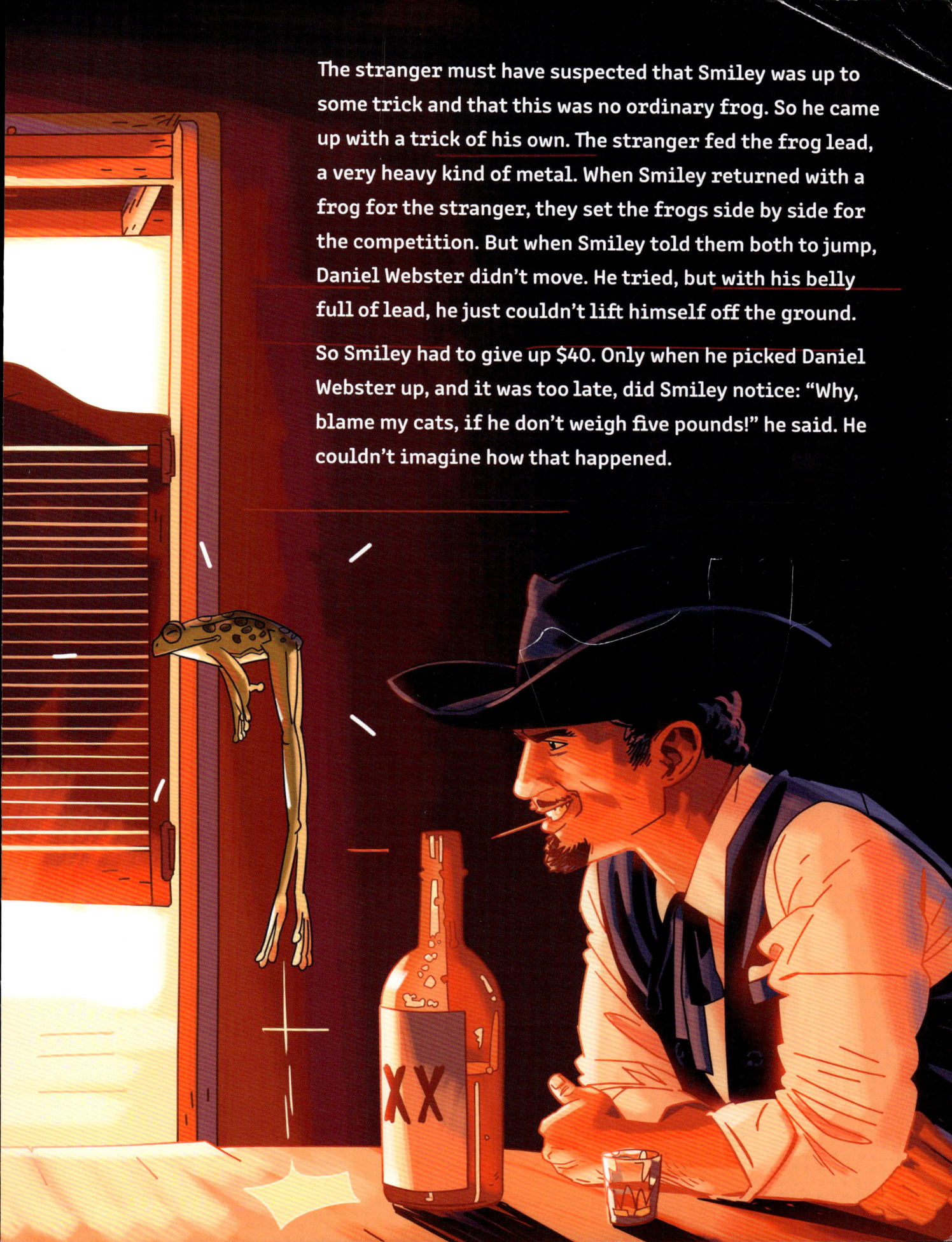

The stranger must have suspected that Smiley was up to some trick and that this was no ordinary frog. So he came up with a trick of his own. The stranger fed the frog lead, a very heavy kind of metal. When Smiley returned with a frog for the stranger, they set the frogs side by side for the competition. But when Smiley told them both to jump, Daniel Webster didn't move. He tried, but with his belly full of lead, he just couldn't lift himself off the ground.

So Smiley had to give up $40. Only when he picked Daniel Webster up, and it was too late, did Smiley notice: "Why, blame my cats, if he don't weigh five pounds!" he said. He couldn't imagine how that happened.

After *The Celebrated Jumping Frog of Calaveras County*, Mark Twain's talent for writing became so famous that he secured a place on a dream tour across the Atlantic Ocean and all around the Mediterranean Sea—all in exchange for writing about it.

In those days, when there were no movies, no internet, no television, and no radio, travel books were the only way most people learned about other countries.

Imagine what it was like for people to read about all those famous places— Rome, Paris, the ruins of ancient Greece, and even the city of Jerusalem that they had read about in the Bible.

Of course, Mark Twain didn't just describe those places. He made them come alive.

ROME

GREECE

He also made fun of everything that everyone else took seriously.

Here's how he let the readers know that his American colleagues just didn't realize how badly they spoke French:

"In Paris, they just simply opened their eyes and stared when we spoke to them in French! We never did succeed in making those idiots understand their own language."

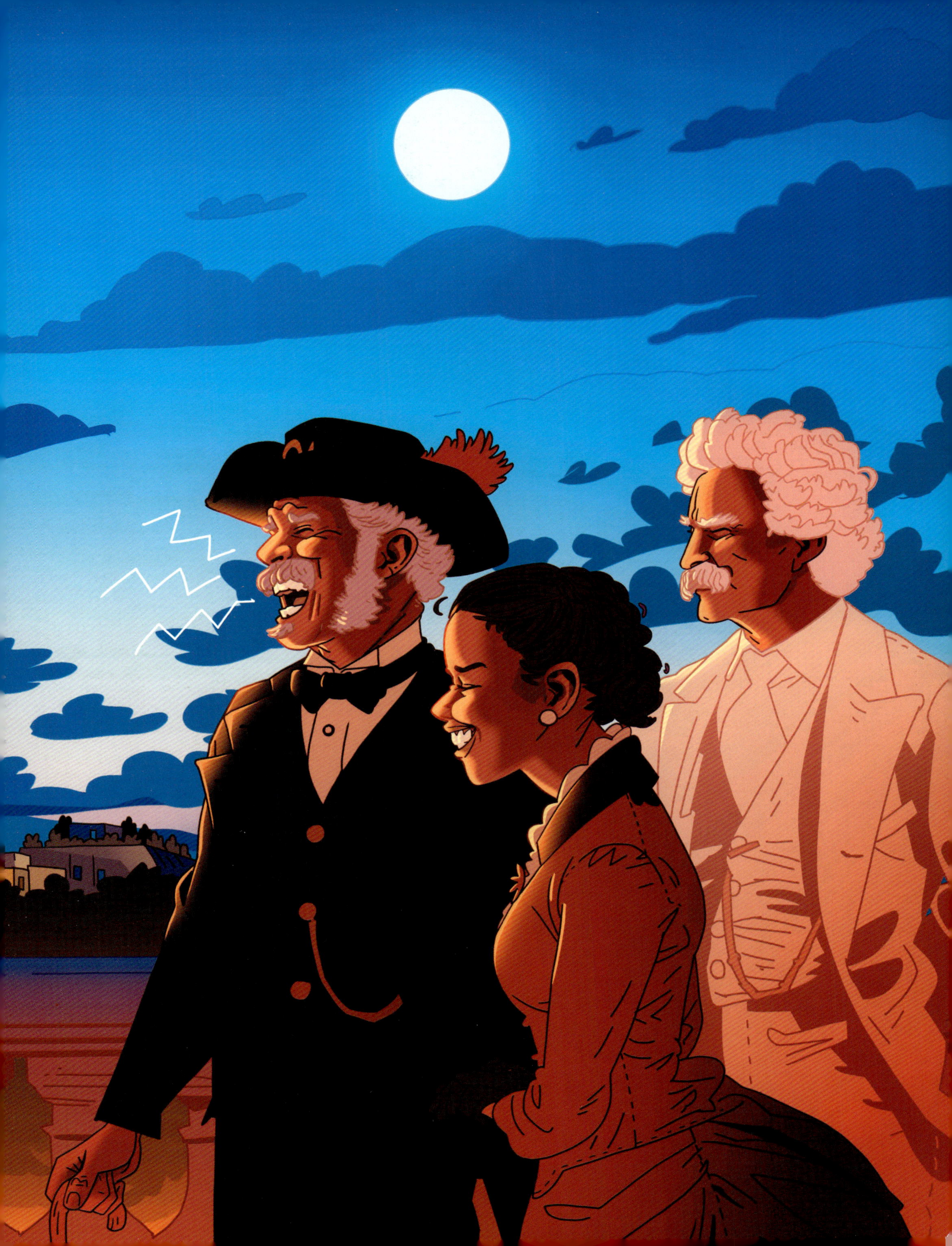

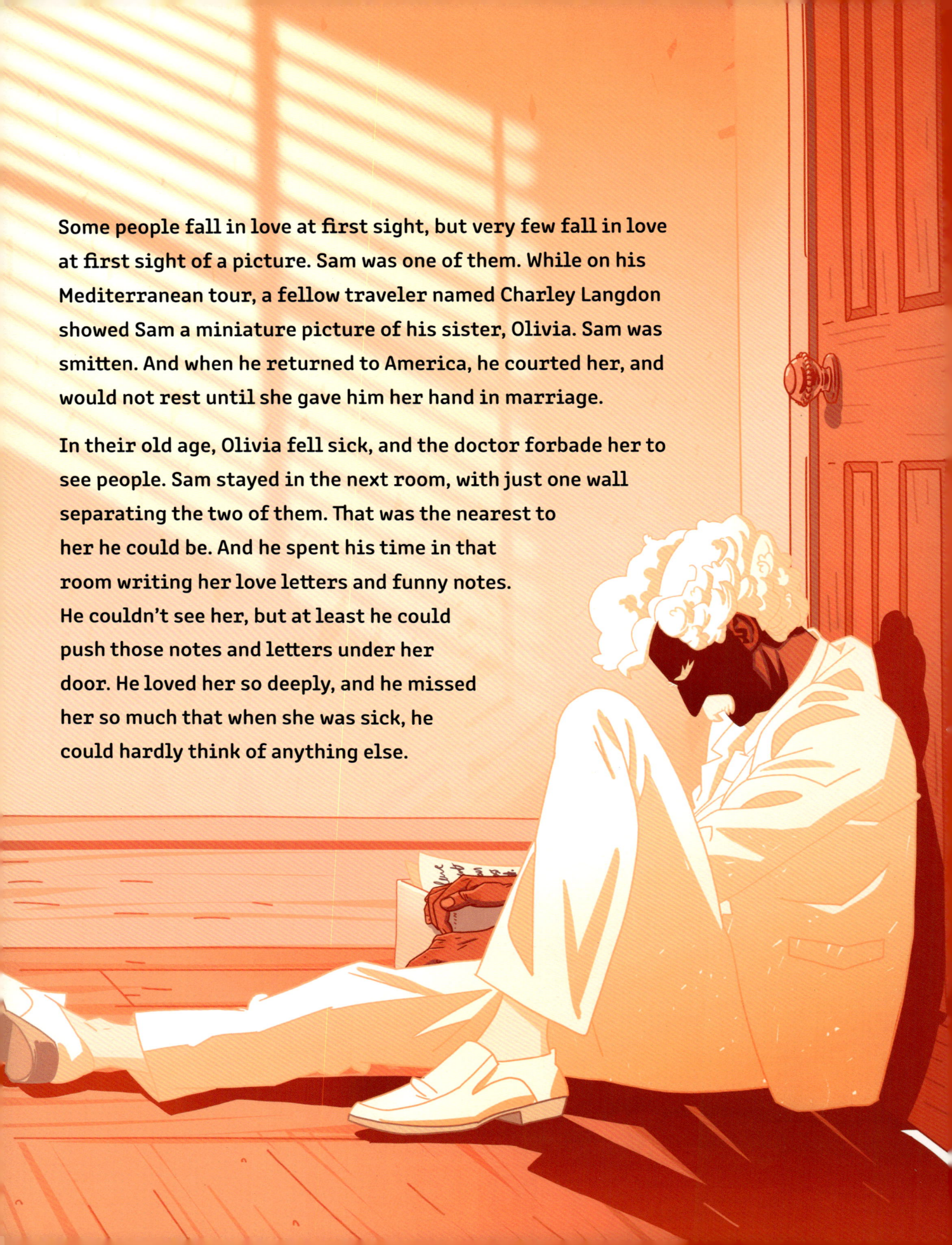

Some people fall in love at first sight, but very few fall in love at first sight of a picture. Sam was one of them. While on his Mediterranean tour, a fellow traveler named Charley Langdon showed Sam a miniature picture of his sister, Olivia. Sam was smitten. And when he returned to America, he courted her, and would not rest until she gave him her hand in marriage.

In their old age, Olivia fell sick, and the doctor forbade her to see people. Sam stayed in the next room, with just one wall separating the two of them. That was the nearest to her he could be. And he spent his time in that room writing her love letters and funny notes. He couldn't see her, but at least he could push those notes and letters under her door. He loved her so deeply, and he missed her so much that when she was sick, he could hardly think of anything else.

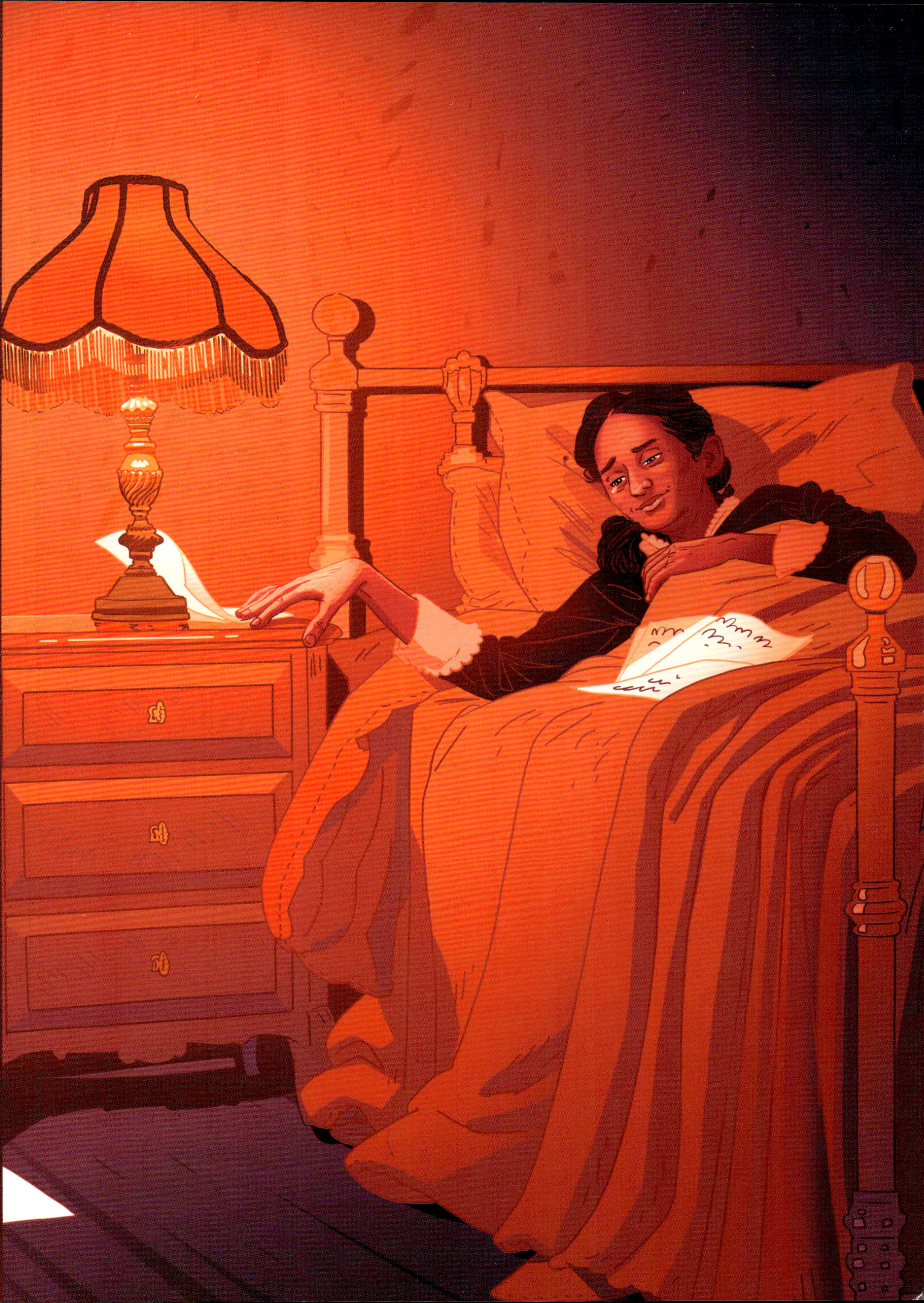

Halley's Comet appears in Earth's sky once in every 75 years, as it travels around the sun, with its beautiful, luminous tail. Samuel Langhorne Clemens was born shortly after Halley's Comet graced Earth's sky, in 1835.

Sam predicted that he would leave this world with Halley's Comet, just as he had come into it. And he was right. He passed away the day after Halley's Comet made its closest approach to Earth, on April 21, 1910. It was as if Sam's life, like a story, ended with a period.

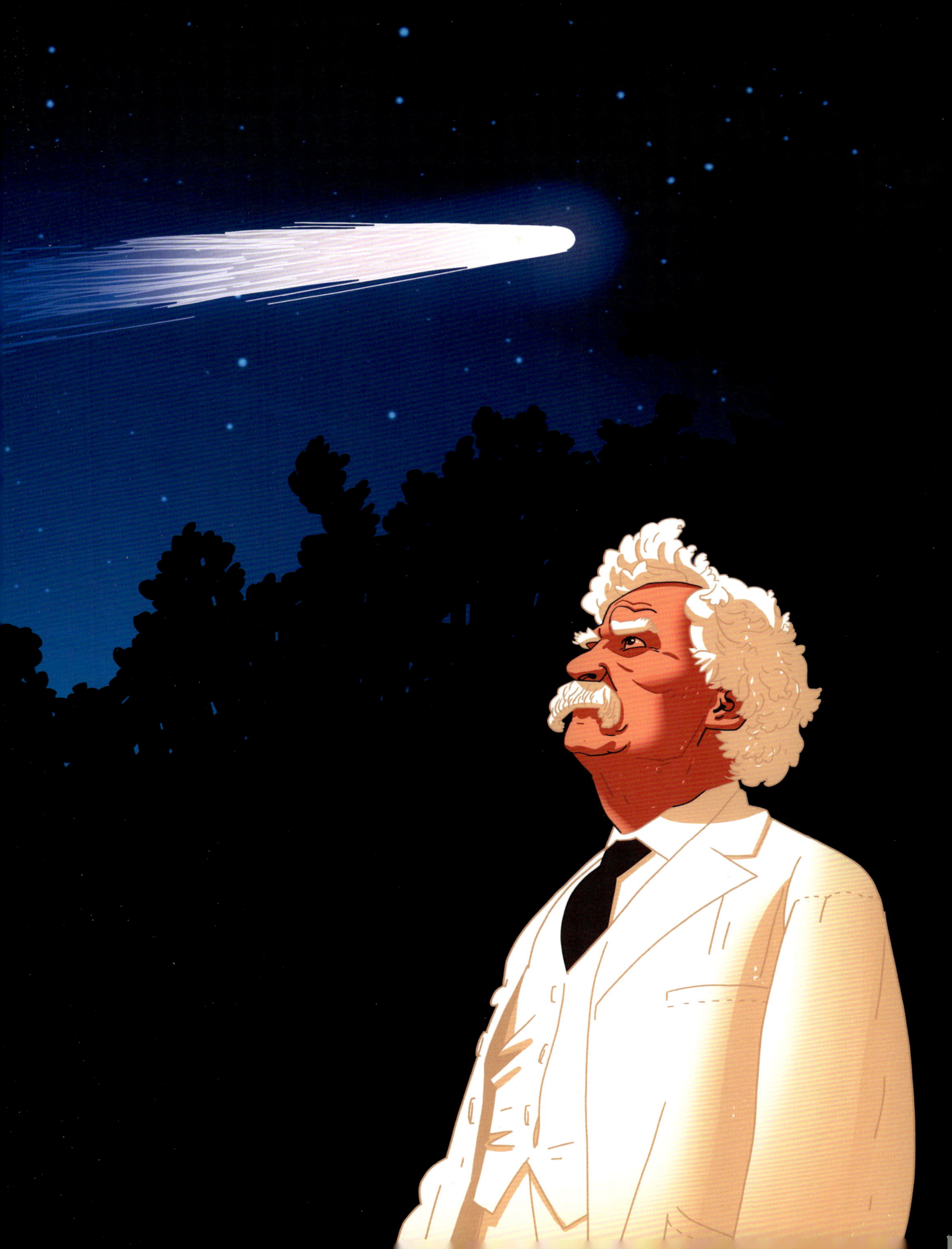

In his old age, Mark Twain became the most famous living American. He was even President Theodore Roosevelt's guest in the White House. He was invited to give lectures around the world, and upon his return, crowds would gather to see the famous man disembark the ship that had carried him home. People would congregate to hear him speak, and readers would await every fruit of his pen.

Samuel Clemens himself is no longer with us, but Mark Twain's books are part of our national treasures. You may read his work alone under the small light above your bed, at your desk, or under a tree outside. But you are not really alone. In reading him, you join the great American experience of generations past, and of many, many American generations to come.

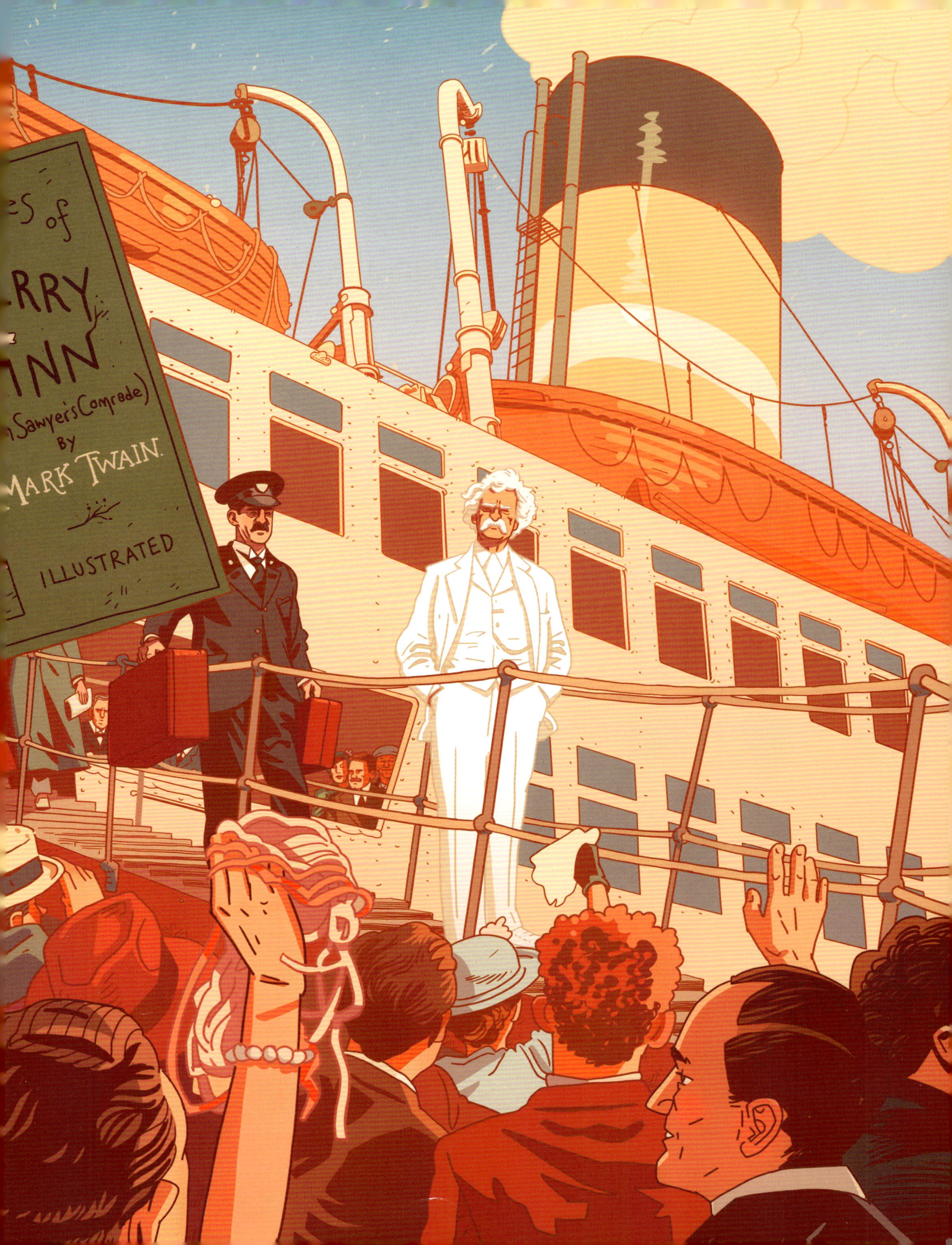

es of
RRY
INN
Sawyer's Comrade)
BY
MARK TWAIN.
ILLUSTRATED

7 INTERESTING FACTS ABOUT Mark Twain

MARK TWAIN LOST A LOT OF MONEY INVESTING IN TECHNOLOGICAL INNOVATIONS THAT CAME TO NOTHING. HE USUALLY RECOVERED MUCH OF IT, BY WRITING BESTSELLING BOOKS.

HE LEFT SCHOOL AFTER FIFTH GRADE. HE LATER EDUCATED HIMSELF IN PUBLIC LIBRARIES.

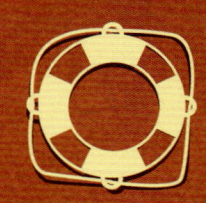

HE WAS A PASSENGER ABOARD A STEAMSHIP THAT RESCUED THE SURVIVING CREW OF A WRECKED SHIP, IN THE MIDDLE OF THE ATLANTIC. HE WROTE A MOVING ACCOUNT OF THE RESCUE.

HE WROTE A BOOK ABOUT A MODERN AMERICAN WHO TRAVELED BACK IN TIME. IT IS CALLED "A CONNECTICUT YANKEE IN KING ARTHUR'S COURT."

HE AND HIS WIFE OLIVIA HAD FOUR CHILDREN.

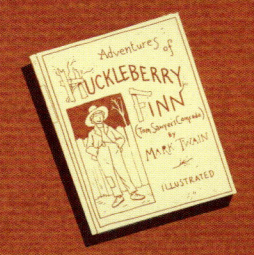

THE FAMOUS AMERICAN NOVELIST, ERNEST HEMINGWAY SAID THAT "ALL MODERN AMERICAN LITERATURE COMES FROM ONE BOOK BY MARK TWAIN CALLED HUCKLEBERRY FINN."

HE BELIEVED HUMOR WAS A GREAT WAY TO LOOK AT LIFE--EVEN AT SAD THINGS.

Mark Twain Said...

> "Anger is an acid that can do more harm to the vessel in which it is stored than to anything on which it is poured.

> Age is an issue of mind over matter. If you don't mind, it doesn't matter.

> Action speaks louder than words, but not nearly as often.

Mark Twain Said...

> "Patriotism is supporting your country all the time, and your government when it deserves it.

> "The reports of my death have been greatly exaggerated.

> "Wrinkles should merely indicate where smiles have been.